LEVEL
3

READER

WITHDRAWN

For kids everywhere who dream big —K. J.

Designed by Yay! Design

Names: Jazynka, Kitson, author. | National Geographic Kids (Firm), publisher. | National Geographic Society (U.S.)
Title: Buzz Aldrin / by Kitson Jazynka.
Description: Washington, DC : National Geographic Kids, [2019] | Series: National geographic readers | Audience: Ages 6-9. | Audience: K to grade 3.
Identifiers: LCCN 2018031434 (print) | LCCN 2018035245 (ebook) | ISBN 9781426332081 (e-book) | ISBN 9781426332098 (e-book+audio) | ISBN 9781426332074 (hardcover) | ISBN 9781426332067 (pbk.)
Subjects: LCSH: Aldrin, Buzz--Juvenile literature. | Project Apollo (U.S.)--Juvenile literature. | Apollo 11 (Spacecraft)--Juvenile literature. | Astronauts--United States--Biography--Juvenile literature. | Space flight to the moon--Juvenile literature.
Classification: LCC TL789.85.A4 (ebook) | LCC TL789.85.A4 J39 2019 (print) | DDC 629.45/0092 [B] --dc23
LC record available at https://lccn.loc.gov/2018031434

The author and publisher gratefully acknowledge the literacy review of this book by Mariam Jean Dreher, professor of reading education, University of Maryland, College Park.

Photo Credits

Cover, NASA; header, Lauritta/Shutterstock; vocab art, NASA; 1, NASA; 3, Bonhams/Barcroft Media/Getty Images; 4-5, NASA; 6-8, Courtesy of the Buzz Aldrin Photo Archive; 9, Aviation History Collection/Alamy Stock Photo; 10, Lee Balterman/The LIFE Images Collection/Getty Images; 11, IM_photo/Shutterstock; 12, Courtesy of the Buzz Aldrin Photo Archive; 13 (UP), Ted Spiegel/Getty Images; 13 (LO), Courtesy of the Buzz Aldrin Photo Archive; 14, Pete Hoffman/Shutterstock; 15, Courtesy of the Buzz Aldrin Photo Archive; 16 (UP), Paul Popper/Popperfoto/Getty Images; 16 (LO), AFPAA/U.S. Air Force; 17, NASA; 18 (UP), Ralph Morse/The LIFE Picture Collection/Getty Images; 18 (LO), Hilary Andrews/NG Staff; 19 (UP LE), MediaPunch/REX/Shutterstock; 19 (UP RT), Bobby Bank/WireImage/Getty Images; 19 (LO), NASA; 20, NASA; 21, Ralph Morse/The LIFE Picture Collection/Getty Images; 22-25, NASA; 26 (UP), PremiumVector/Shutterstock; 26 (LO), NASA; 27-33, NASA; 34 (1), NASA; 34 (2), Charles & Anne Lindbergh/National Geographic Creative; 34 (3), ABC Photo Archives/ABC via Getty Images; 35 (4), Corbis/Corbis via Getty Images; 35 (5), Image Science and Analysis Laboratory, NASA-Johnson Space Center; 35 (6), Kevin Mazur/Getty Images; 35 (7), Ron Galella/Getty Images; 36 (UP), NASA; 36 (LO), Charles Tasnadi/AP/REX/Shutterstock; 37, Courtesy the Buzz Aldrin Photo Archive; 38, Dimitrios Kambouris/Getty Images for WE; 39, Shelby Lees/NG Staff; 40-43 (timeline), Castleski/Shutterstock; 40, Emory Kristof/National Geographic Creative; 41, Lev Fedoseyev/TASS via Getty Images; 42, Paul Buck/Epa/REX/Shutterstock; 43, NASA/JPL/University of Arizona/National Geographic Creative; 44 (1), International News Photos/Underwood Archives/Getty Images; 44 (2), AP Photo; 44 (3), NASA; 45 (4-6), NASA; 45 (7), Somchai Som/Shutterstock; 46 (UP), Image Source/Getty Images; 46 (CTR LE), SSPL/Getty Images; 46 (CTR RT), NASA; 46 (LO LE & LO RT), NASA; 47 (UP LE), NASA; 47 (UP RT), Hilary Andrews/NG Staff; 47 (CTR LE), NASA; 47 (CTR RT), Johan Swanepoel/Shutterstock; 47 (LO LE & LO RT), NASA

National Geographic supports K–12 educators with ELA Common Core Resources. Visit natgeoed.org/commoncore for more information.

Printed in the United States of America
18/WOR/1

Table of Contents

Who Is Buzz Aldrin?

Buzz Aldrin is a famous astronaut.
In 1969, he flew to the moon on a
mission (MIH-shun) called Apollo 11.

That mission made history when he and
another astronaut walked on the moon.
Afterward he blasted back to Earth to
share what he'd learned. Since then,
Aldrin has devoted his life to studying
space travel and teaching others about it.

In His Own Words

"Shoot for the moon; you
might get there."

UNITED STATES

Buzzer

Edwin Aldrin, Jr., was born on January 20, 1930. He grew up in Montclair, New Jersey, U.S.A.

Aldrin as a boy

When he was a toddler, everyone in his family called him Brother. His sister Fay Ann couldn't pronounce the word "brother." She called him Buzzer instead. So his family gave him a new nickname: Buzz.

Buzz (front row) posed for this picture with (from left) his mother, his sister Fay Ann, his grandmother, his sister Madeline, his cousin Gretel, and his aunt Madeline.

That's a FACT!

Before she was married, Aldrin's mother's last name was Moon.

Aldrin and his father in 1944

Aldrin's father was an officer in the U.S. Air Force. He flew airplanes. When Aldrin was two years old, his father took him on his first airplane ride. They flew in a small white plane with a red eagle painted on it.

Young Aldrin was scared. But he loved the thrill of flying through the sky. He didn't know yet that one day he'd fly through the sky on a much bigger adventure.

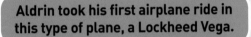
Aldrin took his first airplane ride in this type of plane, a Lockheed Vega.

Big Dreams

Aldrin was smart and quick. Growing up, he played football and learned to pole-vault (POLE-vawlt). He also swam. Most of all, he liked to compete … and win!

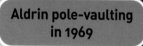

Aldrin pole-vaulting in 1969

Aldrin loved talking with his father about flying and the mystery of space travel. When Buzz was a boy, scientists were just beginning to understand how to reach space. They were still trying to build a rocket that could blast out of Earth's atmosphere. Space was an unexplored place.

Word to Know

ATMOSPHERE: The layer of air that surrounds a planet, separating it from outer space

Aldrin at West Point

After high school, Aldrin went to college at the U.S. Military Academy at West Point. His goal was to be a pilot in the U.S. Air Force. He studied hard and graduated at the top of his class.

Aldrin had bigger dreams, too. He wanted to fly into outer space. At the time, no human had traveled that far. But scientists were getting close. By 1950, they had sent fruit flies, a mouse, and several monkeys into space.

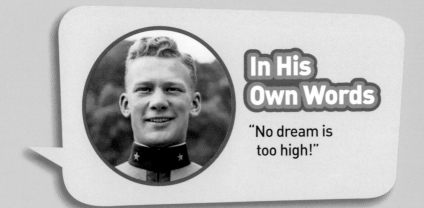

In His Own Words

"No dream is too high!"

Taking Flight

In 1951, Aldrin joined the Air Force and learned to fly fighter jets. He loved the thrill of flying fast and free above Earth.

For his service during the Korean War, Aldrin received a high military honor called the Distinguished (dis–TING–gwisht) Flying Cross. But Aldrin still wondered what it would be like to fly into space.

the Distinguished Flying Cross

Aldrin sitting in the cockpit of a fighter jet at Bryan Air Force Base, in Texas, U.S.A.

After the war, Aldrin served for three years in Germany as a flight commander. He flew new, fast F-100 fighter jets. Still, he longed to fly even faster and farther. A friend suggested he'd make a great astronaut.

When Aldrin returned to the United States, he went back to school to earn his doctorate. He studied everything he could about the science of space travel and exploration. He shared his ideas, such as new ways for two spacecraft to join up while in motion.

APOLLO 11

Words to Know

DOCTORATE: The highest degree awarded by a university

SPACECRAFT: A vehicle used to travel in outer space

Gemini 6 and Gemini 7 were the first U.S. spacecraft to join up while flying in space.

Aldrin's Cool Firsts

Buzz Aldrin was the first to do a lot of things. Did you know these firsts?

Aldrin was an astronaut on Apollo 11, the first crewed mission to land on the moon.

Aldrin was the first NASA astronaut with a doctorate to fly into space.

Word to Know

NASA: National Aeronautics and Space Administration; the U.S. agency in charge of space travel and research

Aldrin was the first astronaut to model on the runway at New York Fashion Week.

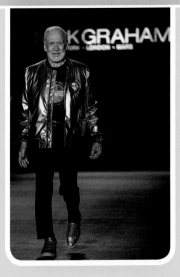

In 2008, Aldrin was among the first group of people honored in the New Jersey Hall of Fame.

During his first space mission, Aldrin took this picture of himself. It was the first "space selfie"!

CHANGE MAG. COCKE

Into Space

In 1963, Aldrin reached his dream of becoming a NASA astronaut. Part of an astronaut's training is learning how to move around in space, where there's little gravity. By practicing underwater, Aldrin learned how walking or using tools would feel in microgravity.

In 1966, Aldrin finally got the chance to fly into space. He and an astronaut named James Lovell set off on the Gemini 12 mission.

Microgravity

In space, there's very little gravity, the force that pulls objects toward the center of a star, planet, or moon. Some call it zero gravity, but that's not quite true. Even far out in space, there is some gravity, just not much. That little bit of gravity is called microgravity. It's part of the reason people and objects seem weightless.

Aldrin (front left) training for microgravity in 1964

The Gemini 12 spacecraft in orbit above Earth

Aldrin and Lovell flew out of Earth's atmosphere. Once they were orbiting Earth, Aldrin got out his ruler and watched it float around inside the spacecraft.

Later, Aldrin performed three space walks. During the second, he floated outside the spacecraft while attached by a tether. Aldrin photographed Earth below and the stars he saw.

In all, he was outside the spacecraft for five and a half hours. That was longer than anyone else at that time.

Aldrin outside the spacecraft during one of his space walks

To the Moon

By 1969, Aldrin had been chosen for a new mission: Apollo 11. The goal was to land astronauts on the moon for the first time and return them safely to Earth.

On July 16, the day of the launch, Aldrin strapped himself into the spacecraft. Next to him were astronauts Neil Armstrong and Michael Collins. The craft rocketed into space.

Spectacular Spacecraft

The Apollo 11 craft was made up of three main parts:

1. A rocket called Saturn V, which powered the craft into space

3. The lunar module, called *Eagle,* which was used to land on the moon

2. The command module, named *Columbia,* in which the astronauts traveled

Once the craft reached space, Saturn V dropped away, and *Columbia* and *Eagle* continued toward the moon. While *Columbia* orbited the moon, *Eagle* separated and landed on the moon's surface. Then part of the lunar module brought the astronauts back to *Columbia.* Only *Columbia* returned to Earth.

Word to Know

LUNAR MODULE: A small craft used to travel between the moon and the main spacecraft

During the flight, the astronauts rested and ate freeze-dried foods like chicken salad and applesauce.

The spacecraft reached the moon on July 19 and started orbiting it. The plan was for Collins to stay in *Columbia* while Aldrin and Armstrong went to the moon's surface.

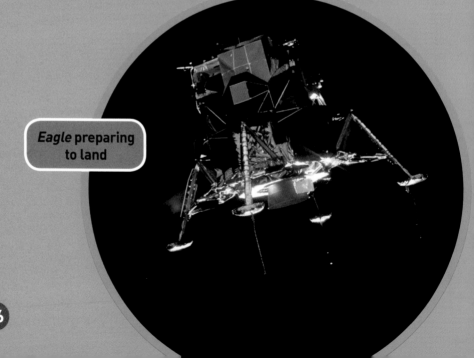

Eagle preparing to land

Space Suits

A space suit protects an astronaut from extreme temperatures. It also provides air to breathe outside the spacecraft. The suit that Aldrin wore to explore the moon weighed 180 pounds. It was made of 25 layers of material. It also had gloves and a helmet with a visor. Aldrin got in and out of the suit through a sealed zipper in the back.

PGA 076

On Sunday, July 20, Aldrin and Armstrong launched *Eagle.* They landed on the surface, then were supposed to rest. But they were too excited to sleep. They were farther away from Earth than humans had ever been. Instead, they put their space suits on. It took them more than four hours! Finally, they secured their helmets and opened the hatch.

Word to Know

APOLLO 11

HATCH: A small door or opening in a spacecraft

When Aldrin climbed down *Eagle*'s ladder, it was hard to balance in his heavy space suit. He stepped onto the moon, then turned around to see the landscape. He described it to those watching on TV on Earth. About 530 million people were watching the adventure, thanks to a special camera and a powerful antenna on the lunar module.

Aldrin climbs down *Eagle*'s ladder and stands on the surface of the moon.

In His Own Words

"Beautiful, beautiful. Magnificent desolation."

—Aldrin describing the surface of the moon

Word to Know

DESOLATION: Emptiness

Exploring the moon was a dangerous job. If one of the astronauts ripped his space suit, he might die. Aldrin and Armstrong stayed together for safety.

That's a FACT!

When he was on the moon, Aldrin thought it smelled like burned charcoal.

Moon Rocks

You can see real moon rocks at the California Science Center in Los Angeles, U.S.A., and at the American Museum of Natural History in New York City, U.S.A. At the National Air and Space Museum in Washington, D.C., U.S.A., you can see a moon rock and also touch it!

They explored the surface for two hours and 15 minutes. They collected 46 pounds of moon rocks to bring home. They also took pictures and checked *Eagle* for damage. They put up an American flag and saluted it. Aldrin felt proud.

When Aldrin and Armstrong were done exploring, they climbed back into *Eagle*. They rocketed back up to *Columbia*, then boarded the spacecraft for the trip home.

On July 24, *Columbia* splashed down in the Pacific Ocean about 1,000 miles from Hawaii, U.S.A. The Navy's U.S.S. *Hornet* picked up the spacecraft and its crew. They were quarantined (KWOR–un–teend) for three weeks, just in case they had brought back germs from the moon.

Word to Know

QUARANTINE: To keep a person away from others in order to stop disease from spreading

After landing, the Apollo 11 crew boarded a raft piloted by a member of the Navy. They waited by *Columbia* for the U.S.S. *Hornet*.

The silver trailer where the Apollo 11 crew was quarantined is on display at a museum in Chantilly, Virginia, U.S.A.

HORNET + 3

President Richard Nixon welcomes the Apollo 11 crew home. The crew has been quarantined inside a trailer.

7 COOL FACTS
About Buzz Aldrin

1

The first time Aldrin applied to become a NASA astronaut, he was turned down—but that didn't stop him from trying again.

2

As a kid, Aldrin spent time with famous pilots Charles Lindbergh and Orville Wright, who were friends with his father.

Charles Lindbergh

Aldrin's childhood hero was the Lone Ranger, a brave fictional cowboy who fought outlaws and rode a horse named Silver.

3

4 After returning from the Apollo 11 mission, Aldrin received the Presidential Medal of Freedom from President Richard Nixon.

Aldrin (far left) with President Nixon (far right)

The Aldrin crater on the moon and the asteroid 6470 Aldrin are named after him.

Aldrin crater

5

6 Aldrin worked with hip-hop artist Snoop Dogg to record a song called "Rocket Experience."

7 In 1988, Aldrin changed his legal name from Edwin to Buzz.

Life on Earth

Aldrin worked with NASA for almost eight years. When he left NASA in 1971, he had logged 289 hours and 53 minutes in space.

Aldrin in 1979, at a ceremony to celebrate the 10th anniversary of the Apollo 11 moon landing

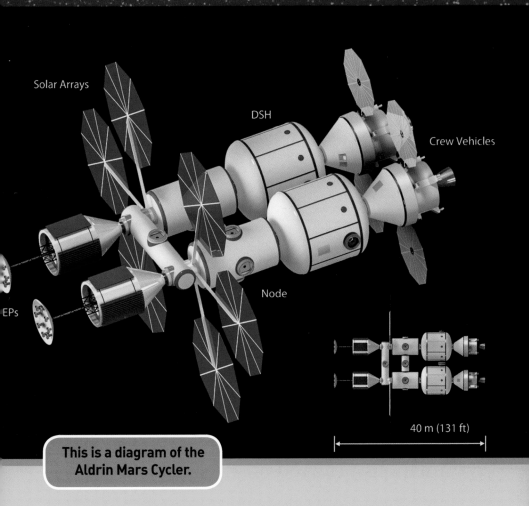

Solar Arrays

DSH

Crew Vehicles

EPs

Node

40 m (131 ft)

This is a diagram of the Aldrin Mars Cycler.

But after leaving NASA, Aldrin didn't quit working. He returned to the Air Force to oversee its test pilot school. He also designed a spacecraft system that could fly to Mars. It's called the Aldrin Mars Cycler.

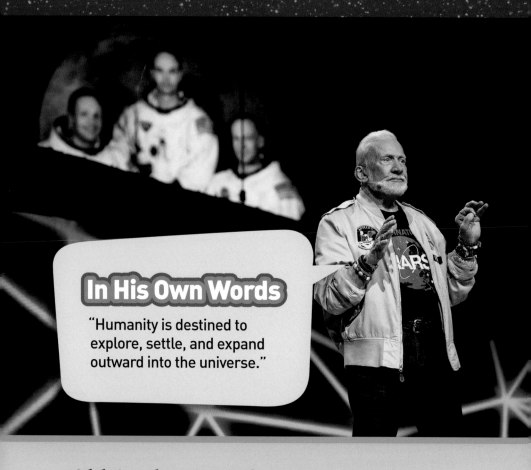

"Humanity is destined to explore, settle, and expand outward into the universe."

Aldrin also started an organization to teach people about space travel. He hopes regular people will get to tour space someday. He also works with schools to inspire children to study science, technology, engineering, math, and art. One day these skills will help people live and work in space.

Aldrin became an author, too. He has written several sci-fi novels, children's books, and memoirs (MEM-wahrz). He has been in movies and made guest appearances on popular TV shows.

Still Exploring

Now Aldrin is an explorer of a different type. Since he retired as an astronaut, Aldrin has explored Earth. He traveled to the ruins of the sunken ship *Titanic* in a mini submarine. He also sailed to the North Pole on an icebreaker ship.

Titanic

1930
Born on January 20 in Montclair, New Jersey

1932
His father takes him on his first airplane ride

1951
Graduates from the U.S. Military Academy at West Point

An icebreaker ship is designed to break through thick ice in Arctic waters.

1953
Is awarded the Distinguished Flying Cross

1963
Earns his doctorate and is accepted into NASA

1966
Completes three space walks, totaling five and a half hours, on the Gemini 12 mission

Stars visible on the Hollywood Walk of Fame:

MARIA CALLAS

GLADYS SWARTHOUT

NEIL A. ARMSTRONG
EDWIN E. ALDRIN JR.
MICHAEL COLLINS
7/20/69
APOLLO
XI

DONALD O' CONNOR

That's a FACT! In 1993, the Apollo 11 crew was honored with four spots on the Hollywood Walk of Fame, in California, U.S.A. Instead of the usual stars, the markers are round like the moon!

1969

Steps onto the moon during the Apollo 11 mission

1969

Receives the Presidential Medal of Freedom

1971

Retires from NASA

Aldrin's dream is for humans to travel to Mars. He believes humans could first reach Phobos, one of Mars's two moons. It's 14 miles wide and orbits about 5,800 miles above Mars. From Phobos, humans could travel back and forth to Mars.

Phobos

Aldrin hopes people from Earth might even be able to *live* on another planet. The most important thing, he says, is never to stop learning or exploring, even if it's just in your backyard.

1998
Travels to the North Pole

2015
Founds the Buzz Aldrin Space Institute in Florida, U.S.A.

QUIZ WHIZ

How much do you know about Buzz Aldrin? After reading this book, probably a lot! Take this quiz and find out.
Answers are at the bottom of page 45.

1

How old was Aldrin when his father took him on his first airplane ride?

A. 2
B. 10
C. 16
D. 62

2

In which war did Aldrin fly fighter jets?

A. the Revolutionary War
B. the Civil War
C. the Korean War
D. the Space War

When did Aldrin become a NASA astronaut?

A. 1930
B. 1963
C. 1969
D. 1988

3

4

How long did Aldrin spend outside the spacecraft during Gemini 12?

A. one hour
B. four hours
C. five and a half hours
D. twelve hours

5

Where did the Apollo 11 mission travel?

A. to the moon
B. to Mars
C. to Phobos
D. to the sun

6

On the Apollo 11 mission, what was *Eagle*?

A. the mascot
B. the lunar module
C. the U.S. Navy rescue ship
D. the rocket

7

What did Aldrin and Armstrong do after landing on the moon?

A. explored the surface for more than two hours
B. collected 46 pounds of moon rocks
C. put up an American flag and saluted it
D. all of the above

Answers: 1. A; 2. C; 3. B; 4. C; 5. A; 6. B; 7. D

Glossary

ATMOSPHERE: The layer of air that surrounds a planet, separating it from outer space

HATCH: A small door or opening in a spacecraft

LUNAR MODULE: A small craft used to travel between the moon and the main spacecraft

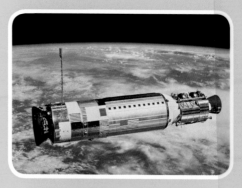

QUARANTINE: To keep a person away from others in order to stop disease from spreading

SPACECRAFT: A vehicle used to travel in outer space

DESOLATION: Emptiness

DOCTORATE: The highest degree awarded by a university

NASA: National Aeronautics and Space Administration; the U.S. agency in charge of space travel and research

ORBIT: To move in a path around another object, such as a star or planet

SPACE WALK: An activity in which an astronaut spends time outside a spacecraft while in space

TETHER: A line, such as a rope or chain, that is attached to something to keep it in a particular area

Boldface indicates illustrations.